Dea[r]

Tc

western hiking

xox

maddy ;Harr[i]

Grand Canyon

Gregory McNamee, SERIES EDITOR

BOOKS IN THE SERIES Desert Places

The Black Rock Desert
William L. Fox and Mark Klett

Cedar Mesa
David Petersen and Branson Reynolds

Chiricahua Mountains
Ken Lamberton and Jeff Garton

The Hanford Reach
Susan Zwinger and Skip Smith

Organ Pipe
Carol Ann Bassett and Michael Hyatt

The San Luis Valley
Susan J. Tweit and Glenn Oakley

Grand Canyon
Ann H. Zwinger and Michael Collier

Grand Canyon

Little Things in a Big Place

TEXT BY Ann Zwinger

PHOTOGRAPHS BY Michael Collier

The University of Arizona Press   Tucson

The University of Arizona Press
Text © 2006 Ann H. Zwinger
Photographs © 2006 Michael Collier

∞ This book is printed on acid-free, archival-quality paper.
Manufactured in the United States of America

11 10 09 08 07 06   6 5 4 3 2 1

Library of Congress Cataloging-in-Publication Data appear on
the last printed page of this book.

Frontispiece: Ripples in Marble Canyon, Mile 38

contents

LIST OF PHOTOGRAPHS   ix

ACKNOWLEDGMENTS   xi

Introduction   1

Prologue   5

Time Passes, Circumstances Change, Things Happen   11

BIBLIOGRAPHY   77

photographs

Ripples in Marble Canyon   *frontispiece*

North Canyon pool   18

Espo in Silver Grotto   20

Redwall Limestone framing a Marble Canyon sky   25

Looking out the opening of Redwall Cavern   27

Raft in Marble Canyon dwarfed by sheer walls   29

Dave at Buck Farm Canyon   35

Grass in Buck Farm Canyon   44

Looking upstream at Saddle Canyon   47

Hikers in Chuar Valley   51

Folds in Vishnu Schist near Clear Creek   53

Flood over travertine in Elves Chasm   60

Clouds below Blacktail Canyon   62

Datura in bloom at Havasu   69

Columnar basalt below Lava Falls   73

Hikers at Mile 214   75

PHOTOGRAPHS

X

acknowledgments

This book is a personal compilation of various recent river trips, and a goodly amount of time in Grand Canyon. If I had my way, this acknowledgment would list every river passenger and boatman and swamper and baggage boatman I ever traveled with. Great idea but impractical. I hope I told them at the time of my appreciation for their company, their good humor, their pleasure in the canyon, their wit, and their patience. If not, I hope they will consider themselves thanked here. Being on trips with all of them was my privilege. Grand Canyon brings out the best in all of us.

Michael Collier's beautiful photographs were a joy to work with, as was Michael, always prompt to answer questions, gracious and helpful. I especially thank those who have furnished me with crucial information and/or read the manuscript and proffered thoughtful editorial comments, marvelous and kindly colleagues all: Mike Buchheit, Jane Cauvel, Brad Dimock, Judy Durzo, Joachim Gottwald, Dan Hall, Kristin Huisinga, Cathy Lowis, Lori Makarick, Scott Mosiman, Patricia Musick, Lance Newman, Andre Potochnik, Charlotte Rixon, Sara Roberts, J. P. Running, Richard Quist, Christa Sadler, Kate Watters, Greg Woodall, Jane Zwinger, and Susan Zwinger. My particular thanks to my live-in techie who got me through the technical requirements of today's manuscript submission.

I would be remiss if I did not thank those who made it possible to spend so much time "down there": Patti Hartmann and Harrison Shaffer, at the University of Arizona Press, and, particularly, Gregory McNamee, who's always talking me into book projects—thank heavens!

Thanks to copyeditor John Mulvihill, any errors are mine, and any omissions of thanks are painfully mine, for no one ever writes a book alone.

introduction

Inconceivable that anyone picking up a book about Grand Canyon doesn't already know where it is. Were it marketable real estate, it would exemplify the classic "location location location," a river plunked right in the middle of the most stunning landscape in the American West. The Colorado River, which reamed out the canyon, begins above Grand Lake in Colorado and runs (theoretically, at least) to the Gulf of California, some 1,450 miles; of that, Grand Canyon proper begins at Glen Canyon Dam and continues 276 miles to the Grand Wash Cliffs at the upper end of Lake Mead, neatly slicing off the northwest corner of Arizona and running through two major deserts, Great Basin and Sonoran, and snacking on a corner of a third, the Mojave. Grand Canyon is famous for its rapids and memorable river trips, its incredible scenery, unparalleled geological exposures of sedimentary layers and stunning walls of volcanic basalt columns, unique hikes, and always, *always*, the harmonies of a river following its fate downstream: sometimes raucous and boisterous, but often pensive, musing, calming, believable, reality at its best.

In the ensuing pages, canyons, rapids, beaches, and all places of interest are identified by mile and whether "R" or "L" (right or left) looking *downstream*, a practice begun in 1923 by the Birdseye Expedition, on the lookout for dam sites. When there's no "Fourth and Main," no "I-40 Exit 334," the only way to identify where you are is by miles. It's taken me a while to achieve that sense of sequence that I find so pleasantly stabilizing; I *like* anticipating the next remembered delight or bracing for the next inundation. All written river guides record miles, and so will this book.

The showy places in Grand Canyon exude a huge physical presence. You count them on your river rosary, beginning with the first rapid at Badger Creek, through Marble Canyon and the Granite Gorges, all the way to the Grand Wash Cliffs. But there are also the small personal mementos: a row of datura flowers in magnificent bloom; red waterfalls shooting over a cliff edge after a big rain on the rim as if from fire hoses; eight slender bighorn sheep, drinking at water's edge, standing so still for so long they look like sculpture; finding the perfect, elegant, deserted beach; rain orchestrating the river's surface; listening to the Great Unconformity and the stories it tells. For me, such quiet moments, unexpected, precise, extraordinary, come to mind more often and more poignantly than the flashy boom-and-crescendo, well-advertised big-time views.

Grand Canyon graces us with both. Communal *and* personal. We can all talk about the big ones, but the personal moments are up to each of us to discover like the perfect river cobble to be held in the hand like an amulet against the winter days to come. It behooves us to take time alone to sit and stare, be attentive, be aware, maybe sketch a special view into memory, for this is a place like no other, and time here is like no other time.

Trust me.

Glen Canyon Dam marks the beginning of Grand Canyon and seems to me to be a good place to start, even though it's not the usual one. River trips begin at Lees Ferry at Mile 0.0, the designated dividing line set by the 1922 Colorado River Compact, while Grand Canyon officially begins at the foot of its headstone, Glen Canyon Dam, 15.6 miles upstream from Lees Ferry. In this narrow reach of river, handsome walls of Navajo Sandstone once defined the sinuous and magnificent Glen Canyon. This was the site on which the Bureau of Reclamation chose to build Glen Canyon Dam in 1956.

Leaving from the base of the dam itself is no longer easy because of security, but it can be done under special arrangement. In April 2004, under the auspices of Glen Canyon National Recreational Area, Grand Circle Field School (GCFS) is taking students to study the dam and its effects. I, like most everyone else, have seen many pictures of the dam, but they are postage stamps compared to its massive presence. From the air it's an exquisite miniature model, taken in with a single glance. From a raft, immediately beneath the dam, you have to crane your neck to be able to scan the height and width of its elegant sweeping curve. A delicate rectilinear tracery outlines each block of the 10 million tons of concrete poured here, and endows its facade with great visual stability and serenity.

The dam may look serene, but there has probably been no more contentious dam ever built unless it be the Three Gorges Dam in China. Reputable engineers decried the need for it. Boaters and hikers bemoaned the loss of some of the most exquisite canyons anywhere, with evocative names like "Cathedral in the Desert" and "Music Temple." It was already too late. The dam closed in September 1963, and power generation began eleven years later. On June 22, 1980, the reservoir finally filled to its 600-foot-deep maximum, and to its full pool height, with a surface elevation of 3,700 feet.

It reached a temporary elevation of 3,708.4 feet in 1983 when a brimming reservoir nearly overtopped the dam and the forty-one-foot-diameter spillways, eviscerated by cavitation, spewed out their cement linings under the punch of 92,600 cubic feet per second (cfs). (A cubic foot is about eight gallons, and cfs is a volume/time measurement of how many cubic feet pass a chosen point in one second.) Under normal circumstances, run-through on the generators allows a maximum 33,100 cfs, although this figure varies depending on the immediate needs for electricity downstream. Glen Canyon provides peaking power generation that can be brought up to speed quickly (as coal-fired generation cannot) to address high user demands that generally occur early morning and late afternoon.

Geologist Andre Potochnik is present today as one of the GCFS instructors. He tells us that, as of April 2004, Lake Powell is 118 feet below full pool. Andre is one of twenty-four members of the Adaptive Management Work Group, a federal advisory committee representing all the stakeholders that concerns itself with matters of the river; it seeks a consensus on how best to assess, address, and advise administrators on the myriad problems facing Grand Canyon and "to effect positive change." Not a simple task.

Because of a persistent drought, releases from the dam are currently much lower than usual, to forestall a time when perhaps no water can be released downstream because of the danger of silt damaging the delicate fins of the turbines. The twenty-year drought is as severe as that the Ancient Puebloans faced in the 1300s and 1400s. Recorded in tree ring data, the severity of that drought forced them to abandon the Four Corners/Grand Canyon area.

Months after this visit to the dam, the water level was still falling and total outflow exceeded current inflow by 103,168 acre feet. Both snowpack and total precipitation were above average, but the pool level of Lake Powell had fallen 131.59 feet below full pool elevation, containing 37 percent less water than what is considered normal. The Bureau of Reclamation estimated that it would require ten years of average flow to fill Lake Powell again; others say it will never fill again. Truth is, nobody knows. With good runoff from snowpack in the mountains, the lake level can rise quickly. The only constant is change. But one thing does seem apparent: if moisture delivery does not continue past the wet summer of 2004, drought will dramatically affect the lives of domestic and farming communities beholden to Lake Powell's water releases and generating capacity. The drought won't be over until the fat river sings.

Hanging gardens festoon the sandstone cliffs on either side of the river flanking the dam, dripping maidenhair ferns and monkey flowers, tapping into the vast amount of water circulating in the rock known as "bank storage." Seepage discolors the rock, an uneasy reminder of how much water sieves through the porous Navajo Sandstone. Seepage has increased over the years, once reaching more than 1,900 gallons/minute. The pattern of metal squares on the walls marks the drill holes of more than five hundred forty- to eighty-foot-long bolts, cemented into the walls to stabilize them. Huge numbers of thermometers and stress meters and heaven knows what else lie embedded in the dam itself to monitor its health on a minute-to-minute basis.

I am relieved when the boatman points the raft downstream. At the base of the eight turbine outlets, water swirls and roils, clear and green. The clarity of the water is the first thing noticed by people who know the lower river—Colorado Plateau rivers are emphatically *not* "clearwater rivers." Now the dam holds back the normal annual average of 168 million tons of sediment delivered from upstream that built and maintained numerous beaches before dam construction; now very little sediment is available to refurbish those beaches downstream.

Water exits through the base of the dam at 48–50° f, as much as twenty degrees colder than that of the pre-dam river, whose temperatures fluctuated according to season. Now the constant cold water encourages the growth of diatoms and other algae on which aquatic invertebrates feed, and their multiplication nourishes a population of non-native trout that could not exist in the silty, warm pre-dam river. Glen Canyon Dam created at least two new industries: large-scale commercial river running and guiding on one of the world's premier trout streams.

No summary description like this can describe all the past machinations, let alone the current discussions, about what should/will/might happen to the dam. Several groups propose removing the dam and restoring the river; governmental agencies seek better ways to operate and utilize the dam; Grand Canyon boatmen seek to preserve the quality of the river experience; environmentalists are concerned about native species like humpback chub whose population has drastically declined since dam closure. And those are just a few from the considerable list of stakeholders. No one ever promised me that life would be simple, but the complexities presented by Glen Canyon Dam and the Colorado River severely stretch my faith in the human ability to problem solve.

I open my dog-eared, river-spattered copy of Larry Stevens's *The Colorado River in Grand Canyon* to trace the unfamiliar curves of this reach of river. Like an old family Bible, the frayed front page records all the Colorado River trips I've taken. These fifteen miles are brand new to me. The river swings to the right and the dam disappears. Three goldeneyes, crisply patterned in black and white, float peaceably along the river's left bank, migrants stopping on their way north. As our behemoth of a raft approaches, they lift off, short, sturdy, earnest little bodies, lofting themselves upstream. Their silver-dollar-size white cheek patches shine like newly minted coins.

How lovely they are.

time passes, circumstances change, things happen

It makes no difference which outfitter, who is or isn't in charge, the time of day, the length of the river trip, whatever: it always takes around two hours to get the safety talk done and people fitted and snugged into life vests, gear loaded with clangs and bangs and shuddering thunks, carried by boatmen levitating across bouncy pontoons and over shipped oars and open boxes like leafhoppers.

In the mile between Lees Ferry and the Paria Riffle, the first tributary to enter the river, the door to the river opens. A fresh breeze catches me in the face. The small cross riffles smack and warble. Cool vapors lift off the perking water. My blood pressure drops twenty points on the instant. The Paria swirls a banner of cloudy water into the clear green water of the river. Lots of rain upstream recently swept sand and silt down the Paria's desert-dry streambed and reminds the river of its proper café au lait hue. Its silt hisses on the hull of the boat.

Shortly we pull over for the quintessential river lunch: generically the same but always opulent and plentiful and beautifully laid out. While tomato seeds slip down T-shirt fronts and orange peels perfume the air, we listen to another safety talk, the first having been given at Lees Ferry when everyone's life jackets were fitted to suffocation. The boatman-designee for this job begins: "This is a big volume river but a benign river. Some people court being thrown out of a boat as a necessary highlight of the trip. [*Dramatic pause.*] Don't even think about it, folks! The shock of 50° river water is mind-numbing and enervating. Prepare yourself psychologically when you go into a rapid. Think ahead about what you'd do if you suddenly found yourself in the water. A flip happens too fast to think. Immediately, if you're all right, pat the top of your head in the universal signal for "I'm OK!" Be proactive, engage in positive pointing and gesturing. If you're close to the boat, someone can pull you in by grasping the shoulders of your life jacket and giving a mighty heave. Remember all that cinching of straps up to breathless at Lees Ferry? Now you know why: to prevent your jacket from coming off over your head, because then you *really* have a problem. If you're too far away to be hauled in, float on your back with your feet lower than your head. Your regulation life jacket with its big collar is designed to keep you face up. You'll be pulled out quicker than you think. Promise!"

That's a lot of instruction while you're trying to swallow your lunch and keep ghastly images out of the way. A timid voice asks what almost everyone is thinking: "Does anyone ever die in the river?" The answer is a sobering "Yes." Silence.

There are no two ways about it: Grand Canyon *is* a dangerous place. That's why you sign a waiver before you even set foot at Lees Ferry. That may even be why you've come, to catch a glimpse of life with an edge on it, to test your ability to react well in unfamiliar situations. I reflect that I have been more at risk trying to walk across the intersection of Cascade and Uintah in Colorado Springs than I have been on the river. I trust and respect the river. I trust the superb boatmen with whom I ride. I accept risk as part of my life because I cannot imagine a life without it. Anyone who skis, crosses the street, drives cars, walks the dog, climbs mountains, sails ships, or gets up in the morning is at risk. Anyone who goes down a big river full of big rapacious rapids should not do so unawares. It is well to remember that only the river runs easy.

While people are licking cookie crumbs off their fingers and reaching for another candy bar, the questions that passengers have been waiting to ask and felt shy about asking now pepper the air. Because they touch basic concerns, most questions are answered in kindly fashion:

1. On first seeing an elegant dory that, with its slender raked bow and stern, looks like a mere sliver of wood when it's parked near a big wallowy orange supply raft: "I'm going down the river in that?" *[Yes!]*

2. "How many miles are we going to go today?" *[As many as we need to.]*

3. "What do we do if it rains?" *[Rejoice.]*

4. "I notice the boatmen have generators to pump up the rafts. Is there any way to charge up my electric razor?" *[Yes, there's a currant bush at nearly every beach.]*

5. "What if we run out of food?" *[It's called the South Canyon Beach diet.]*

6. "When are they going to take down Glen Canyon Dam?" *[Not for a while, anyway.]*

7. "Where do you, uh, go to the bathroom?" *[Listen carefully to the latrine talk and remember that some of the world's vintage conversations occur while standing in line to use it after breakfast.]*

8. "I can't swim. What happens if I fall out of the boat?" *[Do not worry. Do not panic. You will be fine. You're riding with the best boatmen in the world, bar none, and there will be lots of hands ready to haul you out.]*

Then, as hired-gun naturalist, it's my turn to ask questions:

"Raise your hand if you know your home telephone number? Your work number?" Everyone's hands shoot up.

"Street address?" Same.

"PIN number? Social Security number?" Ninety percent response.

"Do you know ten native trees in your area?" Fewer hands. "Forty native flowers in your neighborhood? Five mammals? Fifteen insects?" Finally no hands.

Things like telephone numbers and street addresses define "home" for most of us. But so also do the sycamores and the spring beauty and the gray fossiliferous limestone and the mosquitoes that share that space with you. (I grew up in Indiana.) Home is a distinctive and precious concept. We define ourselves by where we come from; preliminaries on every river trip, bar none, begin with finding out who comes from where.

My challenge to these boaters, in the coming days, is to make Grand Canyon familiar, become your home by seeing if together we can learn five rock formations, ten trees, twenty flowers, and recognize five plant families, ten vertebrates, fifteen insects. Saying we'll have a communal, nonobligatory listing at the end of the trip elicits moans and groans of "this is our vacation," etc.

But I know something they don't know, because I've happily watched it happen trip after trip. After they stop focusing on absent cell phones and e-mail, become comfortable here, this canyon charms people. Most people are curious and enjoy finding out about where they are, intrigued by new places. When they begin to notice what's around them more closely, they *a priori* become good observers, and good observers go away with a headful of knowledge that will brighten a day, warm a winter. They will quickly learn the names of new plants, what constellations glitter on a bracingly clear cold night, recognize who made the tiny footprints on a cattail-rimmed beach, giggle at the burping of newly sprung red-spotted toads, take endless pictures of flowers. They will surpass these meager numbers of my list with verve, and here, in this entirely new place, they will come to be familiar and on speaking terms with the natives of Grand Canyon. One of the definitions of home is, after all, a place with which we are most familiar. To their surprise, because they have learned the names of familiar plants and animals and rocks in the canyon, they will have discovered another home that will enrich and expand their knowledge of their rim-world home.

Honest.

At North Canyon, Mile 20.5R, I do what I always do when I have a few minutes: inventory plants. Near the mouth of the canyon flourishes a garden that, on an early summer day, burgeons with blooms. Field notebook in hand, I list datura, desert dandelion, salmon-flowered globe mallow, lemon yellow Hooker's evening primrose, prickly poppy, and a disheveled prickly tumbleweed. I continue wandering up the canyon, a sculptural marvel cut into the rose-brown Supai Sandstone. Where the walls rise close together, water has carved a curved concave floor with dramatic swags and walls with crisp foliation patterns that look more like designed bas-relief sculptures than the casual art of nature.

Instead of hiking farther up to the end of the canyon with the rest of the group, I straggle back to my chair on the beach. And a good thing it is. At breakfast a particularly aggressive pair of ravens worked our campsite as ravens often do; one worked the kitchen to check for scraps while the other explored the boats and open boxes. The moment anyone shooed one of them away, they made the shortest flight possible out of the way of trouble and, when no one was watching, materialized right back whence they came, insouciant, infinitely cheeky, infinitely crafty, infinitely patient.

When I return from my walk I discover mayhem. The ravens have pulled almost everything out of my daypack: crostic puzzle book, plastic bags, pencil sack, big envelope, etc., despite the fact that I left it zipped up. I stand there in disbelief. Bernd Heinrich (a raven authority who probably is part raven himself) notes that ravens have hung around humans from prehistoric times and are skilled at caching food and remembering where they hid it; I suspect that at some time these ravens found food in someone's opened pack and now remember that daypacks = food. This is one savvy pair.

So I clean up. Get down notes on the ravens while their behavior is still fresh in my mind. Get organized. Watch the river go by. I realize, with a subtle surprise, that not hiking up to the end of the canyon, which I've always loved, may signal a difference in how I react to the canyon. Am I feeling a reluctance to add more footprints to places I've already been? In a way, irrational, in another way, a message: I've had my beautiful hour in North Canyon, I remember the exquisite pool fed by a thread of water slipping down the wall from the lip of the alcove twenty feet above. That first astonished moment, that unexpected slithering sliver of silver reflected in pure perfection, can never come again.

But it is fused in memory.

At Mile 29L, Silver Grotto begins some fifty feet back from the river with a small pear-shaped pool. At the far end, boatmen rig a safety rope to help with the excessively precipitous and reportedly slippery ascent. Other pools

TIME PASSES
17

North Canyon pool, Mile 20

succeed this one, linked like beads in a necklace. About half of us decide not to go, one of those times when wisdom strikes me as the better part of valor. Envious, I watch Kari grab the rope and, with feet planted wide apart, go up the slick rock like Spider Woman. Somewhat irritably, I go to kick rocks on the beach.

Scott, boatman and chef par excellence, fetches me from my sulk with "There's something you need to see," and marches me to a patch of *orange-flowered* Hooker's evening primrose. Usually they are a distinctive pure bright yellow, identifiable from a distance because of their stalky growth pattern and bright blossoms. Not these — they're as orange as tangerines. I count out about eight dozen four-foot-tall plants within a few feet of the river. Biennials, both last and this year's stalks stand surrounded by a generous sprouting of offshoots. Scott says he's seen these blooming here for several years. Enough are still in bloom that they're being visited by fat, black droning carpenter bees, but, at July's end, most are in seed.

When the sides of the tough four-sided capsules begin to peel back, they expose four double rows of seeds. Because I haven't anything else to do at the moment, I count seeds. I calculate that this patch produces roughly 307,200 seeds, hopefully enough to guarantee their continued existence. They are great pioneers in disturbed soil and they're doing well, but a heavy rainstorm or a big beach-building release from the dam, or seed-hungry mice or birds, could take a toll. I hope this population will survive and pass on its tangerine-flower genes and, in the slow pavane of evolution, eventually become a new named variety or, more miraculously, a brand new species.

Espo in Silver Grotto, Mile 29

According to the plethora of new rosettes, they seem to be doing just fine, thank you very much.

Counting seeds a useless exercise? Perhaps. Counting gives the honest numbers that describe a piece of the world. How much is sufficient, how much produces a balance, how many evening primroses are needed to light a river beach, how many to bring a smile of pleasure, how many smiles to right a day? But you have to count first. And this childlike moment has taught me something: how wonderful it is, here on this river, to ponder the puzzle of how much is enough.

A quick brisk breeze skips up the beach, spins some sand, and sets the dry stems of the evening primroses stridulating. Ah ha, I think, Beaufort scale 2. Lest counting seeds seem an idle and desultory occupation, reflect: this close observation, counting noses so to speak, is how science begins. It's how we measure what's going on, quantify, propose a hypothesis, test it, reach a conclusion on the available data.

That's exactly what Admiral Francis Beaufort did when he was in the British navy two centuries ago, establishing a method still used by mariners. He simply observed the effects of wind on the landscape and developed a scale that could reveal, in rough but useful terms, what the current wind velocity might be. Others adapted Beaufort's methods to windmills and waves and hurricanes (Beaufort's scale only goes up to 72 mph; the U.S. Weather Service says hurricane winds begin at 74 mph). Of course, that information is now gathered by scientific instruments, but the judgment of the human eye, which can instantly take in the variables, with the help of the Beaufort scale, is probably just as helpful and always available. "Smoke rises vertically" indicates dead calm, 1 on the Beaufort scale. Wind that moves smoke but not wind vanes is "light air," or Beaufort 2. Wind that raises dust and loose papers and tweaks small branches has reached "moderate breeze" velocity of 13–18 mph, Beaufort 3. By the time "walking against wind is difficult," you're dealing with a "moderate gale" of 32–38 mph.

Since some of Beaufort's descriptive passages aren't particularly applicable to the river, I accept that my duty, for the next hour, is to attempt to adapt a Beaufort scale for the Colorado River:

1	light air	1–3 mph	Life jackets do not need fastening down (but do it anyway).
2	light breeze	4–7 mph	Feels good on face; wind direction can be determined by holding up a wet finger.
3	gentle breeze	8–11 mph	Wind pleasant on face on warm day, miserable on a cold day.
4	moderate breeze	13–18 mph	Unsecured clothing takes off across beach; hats blow off if not tied on.
5	fresh breeze	19–24 mph	Chop forms on the river; jackets flap; considerable difficulty in pitching tents.
6	strong breeze	25–31 mph	Boatmen mutter about the difficulty of rowing against the wind; plastic dishes with spaghetti on them sail off the table;

hard to walk against the wind; sand billows off the beach in pulses and into your tent; contact lens wearers in duress.

When you reach 7, 8, and 9, you're into gale force winds. If tents were not staked and double-weighted inside, they may sail off over the river, not a pretty sight that engenders quickly launched boats frantically chasing a bloated elephant skipping merrily across the river, always just out of reach, sometimes without a happy ending. Along with the strongest winds go an inability to row, air permeated with sand, and misery, with the only option to find a place to hide from the maelstrom. I've been in these conditions and it's sheer misery.

Beaufort, according to his most recent biographer, Scott Huler, was nothing if not a keen observer and consummate recordkeeper, and well connected in the naturalist community. It was he who recommended a young man named Darwin as a companion to Robert Fitzroy on a proposed three-year voyage on a ship named the *Beagle*. Huler characterizes Admiral Beaufort as a man of endless ingenuity and energy, who believed that "nature, rightly questioned, never lies, and that it is incumbent on us all to get up early in the morning to start formulating the best questions we can, and write down what we learn in a way everyone can understand."

Ah, yes.

Within a short ten river miles—Miles 29 to 39—are strung some of the most prestigious sites/sights on the river: Shinumo Creek and Silver Grotto; the Fence Fault, which crosses the river just after Mile 30 and reveals how a readjustment of layers affects the river corridor; South Canyon with its prehistoric walls and petroglyphs; Vasey's Paradise, Redwall Cavern, and Nautiloid Canyon, all enveloped in John Wesley Powell's name, "Marble Canyon."

When the Redwall slanted up out of the river around Mile 23, it looked anything but distinguished, no hint that only ten miles downriver it would rise to form a high horizon of austere splendor that runs almost the length of the canyon. It angles out of the river, creased, nondescript, crosshatched with wrinkles on its cold gray surface (the Redwall is really *gray*, tinted by the brick red hematite contained in overlying Hermit Shale that drizzles color down the Redwall, turning it salmon red).

Visible from South Canyon, a Gothic arch opens, eroded out of the base of the Redwall cliff. The opening marks Stanton's Cave, named after one of the early surveyors of the river, and is one of many solution caves in that formation. Limestone, essentially calcium carbonate, dissolves easily, and solution caves frequently form where water seeps through limestone.

Smaller grottoes formed at river's edge begin as slots, develop into handholds and hollows and small solution caves in which niches nest within larger niches, sometimes hung with massive crystals. Such solution holes form only at water table level or above. These began forming around 300 million years ago as the Supai Formation sandstones were being laid down on top of the Redwall.

Interconnected tubes honeycomb the Redwall, and when the river cuts these pipes, water shoots out like a gigantic faucet turned on full, as it does from Thunder River above Tapeats Creek, and Vasey's Paradise,

Redwall Limestone framing a Marble Canyon sky, Mile 38

immediately downstream. At Vasey's Paradise, water falls to the river in a splashing, pulsating stream that quivers and nourishes cardinal flowers and watercress, and provides a singular habitat for the endangered Kanab amber snail.

A little over a mile downstream and across the river, the granddaddy of all solution caves, Redwall Cavern, opens its huge maw at Mile 33L. From upstream, the opening to Redwall Cavern appears deceptively small. Boats pulled up at the entrance look like grains of rice. You absorb its lofty spaciousness from the inside, scan a vast ceiling swathed with iridescent spider webs, shuffle in a sandy floor traced with tiny mice prints and ant lion larvae tracings, a magical juxtaposition of the minuscule and the munificently monumental.

Since much of the Redwall Limestone was laid down in quiet seas, it often preserves marine shells. Eleven seas came and went while silts formed the Redwall. These were shallow seas, and the fossils of the animals that lived there, crinoids, horn corals, and brachiopods, were all filter feeders in the clear water that stretched from the now-eroded ancient Appalachian Mountains to Nevada. Near the front of Redwall Cavern, bits of crinoid stems and heads lie embedded in a boulder; the segmented stems connected an anchoring "foot" to a five-parted "head" that ingested minute food particles wafted by its mouth. The five-partite design marks crinoids as members of the still extant echinoderm family that includes starfishes and sea urchins and, still around after some 320 million years, crinoids.

When you stand inside Redwall Cavern and look out to the sunlit wall on

Looking out the opening of Redwall Cavern, Mile 33

the other side of the river, you can see different hued horizontal layers neatly roman-striping the wall. A forty-foot-thick layer of Redwall, about thirty or so feet up from the river, contains alternating light and dark gray beds, formed by alternating limestone and chert layers, the earth colors of a fourteenth-century Florentine artist's palette, restrained and elegant: grisaille, pale gray, pearl gray, charcoal gray, ash, slate. These even layers of limestone formed slowly in such a stable environment that the stripes run for long stretches without a quaver. Geologists estimate that it might take a thousand years to settle out six inches of sediment; the massive weight of overlying deposits further compacted the sediments into these thin, fine-grained layers.

Soon shadows swath the river and dun the colors. A canyon wren pipes its otherworldly descending trill. A brief patch of sunlight sends sequins skittering across the water.

Just another beautiful river afternoon.

In his nonriver life, Dr. Mike Anderson is a scholarly, well-respected river historian and lights many a river trip with "blather" (as he terms it). Today he plans to engage us in a discussion of the latest Grand Canyon Management Plan. The entire 2004 management plan, a monstrous document, can be printed from the Internet, as can be the twenty-page executive summary that Mike holds in his hand.

The Colorado River is an anomaly in American rivers: primarily a recreational river, it runs through a national park that sets the rules for its use. Bigger rivers like the Mississippi and the St. Lawrence are regulated, but as

Raft in Marble Canyon dwarfed by sheer walls, Mile 36

commercial rivers. The Colorado River in Grand Canyon is unique in being a good-sized perennial river that a lot of people like to look at and many like to run, both privately and commercially. Conflicting opinions on usage bring everything from heated discussion to legal suits.

Mike reminds us that before Glen Canyon Dam was built, no serious scientific studies provided baseline data about the river other than what came from a couple of flow gauges. Without baseline records, decisions were made about its future with hardly any knowledge of the river and its dynamics. The only studies of any of the places that would be inundated by the waters of Lake Powell were archaeological salvage studies made by archaeologists from the University of Utah on a desperate run through Glen Canyon. Endangered fish species were known to inhabit the river, but no one knew anything about their populations.

Official recordkeeping did not begin until 1971–72, already too late to observe Paul Ehrlich's distillation of Aldo Leopold's dictum about tinkering: "The first rule of intelligent tinkering is to save all the parts." But you can't save parts when no one knows what the parts are to begin with.

Scientific studies on a broad range of subjects began with an environmental impact statement *after* the dam had closed—the first effort to define the parts done with an interdisciplinary approach. The initial phase started in 1982 and was completed in 1988; the next began in June 1988 and finished November 1, 1991. So few river runners boated the river at this time that the industry that we know today did not exist: by 1948 fewer than a hundred people had traveled down the Grand Canyon; by 1964, 900 had. Passenger numbers increased dramatically over the next six years: by 1970, 10,000 people ran the river; and, in 1972, 16,500 people came, prompting the first "management plan" that froze the number of commercial and private parties at 1972 levels. In 1972, the U.S. Park Service also defined the amount of usage by setting the number of allowable "user days" (one person for one day) and controlling it by the number of reservation slots open to boating companies and the number of permits available to private runners. Word spread very quickly that running the Colorado River in Grand Canyon was a great thing to do. Absolutely right: it *is* a great thing to do, and I daresay that it has made more of a difference in many people's lives than any other outdoor experience except maybe climbing Mount Everest.

Multiple studies on birds, beach deterioration, plant populations, river flows, and debris flows, among others, were carried out under Glen Canyon Environmental Studies, an ambitious program that involved a huge number of scientists. Now some data *do* exist, and help form policy in a way not possible before. The 2004 Grand Canyon Environmental Studies is the latest attempt to address the pressures that have developed, to enable judicious decisions to be made about how the river should be used and by whom, but most important, *how to protect Grand Canyon*. This latest proposal will now go through three months of public comment that began in October 2004, with an anticipated 90,000 comments to be collated and considered. Doubtless any decisions forthcoming will be both condemned and praised for the ongoing "management" of the Colorado River—an oxymoron since no human can factor into account all the activities of an uncontrollable, vastly complex natural world.

The last plan, implemented in 1989, caused a lot of contentious litigation. The same major players exist today: commercial boating companies who want to maintain and expand their permits; private river runners who want an easier permitting system and also more slots. The Hualapai Nation is requesting more permits to run their large motor-driven rafts from Diamond Creek down to Lake Mead, pointing out that most commercial river trips end at Diamond Creek or Whitman Wash shortly downstream and seldom go farther and that their trips fulfill a need. Environmental players want greater protection for endangered plants and animals and terrain, and fewer people. Helicopter company owners want more flight time and corridor access. It's a case of if you please all of the people, you fail.

The 2004 plan states the main issue as the "appropriate level of visitor use consistent with natural and cultural resource protection and visitor experience goals." This is the most basic philosophical issue on which all other proposed policies depend. Almost doubling visitation, as the 2004 management plan proposes to do, somehow does not sound to me like the best way to preserve the river corridor.

Against the clatter of loading boats, Mike exhorts listeners to access the document off the Internet and make comments. Applause is drowned in the big hollow "booms!" of metal box lids slamming down. Neat pyramids of yellow bags on the beach wait to be laded aboard; tangles of faded orange life jackets wait to be donned. Every morning it seems impossible that this unwieldy volume of miscellaneous gear could all fit into so few boats.

And every morning it does.

Prodded by the morning sun, the river busies itself casting bubbles. The dip and rise of oars of the dory in front of us traces silvery lines in the water. Riffles spawn millions of pinprick-size bubbles that cavort across the surface like minute water striders. Sparkle and flicker, rhinestone necklaces, diamond bracelets, little lights like birthday candles looking for a party, a river lively and vivacious. A delightfully coherent day, which makes me feel coherent too.

We land at Buck Farm at Mile 41R. I always look forward to a hike up Buck Farm because the rock we walk on, up, and across is Muav Limestone, a handsome rock that has one wonderful characteristic: its narrow and repeated ledges make good footing and form easy up-and-down steps. The very thin beds look as if they were made of cemented fragments, as indeed they were. For 150–200 million years, erosion ate away at the surface of the Redwall Limestone before the Muav Limestone was laid atop its well-weathered surface, creating an unconformity. As its original thin layers formed, wave action of an ancient Cambrian sea constantly fragmented them almost as they were laid.

On a hot summer's day, the walk up Buck Farm is pleasant, edging across Muav ledges, boulder hopping across a tiny streambed. One huge wall supports tiers of moisture-loving vegetation: delicate red-and-yellow columbine, maidenhair fern, prince's-plume, opulent pods of watercress, and a grandiose Rydberg's thistle with fresh thin green leaves two feet long. Higher than my head, the thistle stalks raise multiple seed heads bearing loose clusters of seeds ready to lift off on the first draft of warm air.

One of the relatively few cottonwoods within the canyon leans precariously, not receiving enough water for its size, while smaller trees like buckthorn and redbud flourish. The ubiquitous coyote willow hangs long narrow leaves like flattened green beans. Native peoples chewed the twigs because they contain salicin, closely related to the analgesic properties of acetylsalicylic acid, aka aspirin.

Rather out of place in all this greenery sits a prickly pear, beset with cochineal bugs. Watching out for the glochids, the very tiny fine spines that are a hundred times worse than the big needles, I carefully pull off a cottony scab that protects the small, flat scale insect beneath. My fingers are immediately stained a dark magenta, a dye that remains on my fingers for several hours and that was widely used by prehistoric as well as historic people. Spaniards nurtured plantations of prickly pear for cochineal; they considered the dye so brilliant and precious that it was used only for royal robes.

A patch of evening primroses that opened last evening remain open because the sun has not yet found and wilted them. Their simple four-petaled flowers are, with mustard family blooms, the only frequent striking four-petaled flowers in the canyon. Learning or teaching plants by family makes sense to me because it's how we learn human families, recognizing the members by their distinctive walks or hair color or speech patterns. There's no way someone on a two-week trip can learn and retain the flora of the inner Grand Canyon (currently reckoned at more than 800 species) and find it of much use when they're back in Minnesota or North Carolina. But you can learn the few signal characteristics that characterize several plant families. As you

Dave at Buck Farm Canyon, Mile 40

become familiar with their trademarks, you can then recognize other relatives wherever you are and enjoy that pleasurable *ah HA!* of recognition.

Several familiar plant families are well represented in the canyon: cactus, pea, and, most particularly, the aster family, "aster" being synonymous with "daisy." It's almost impossible to avoid some kind of acquaintance with the latter; *everybody* recognizes a dandelion. Some of the most efficient plants at dispersing their seeds belong to the aster family: dandelions, salsify, and thistles are professionals at this.

On this beach where we're camped grow three frequent aster family plants: brittlebush, skeletonweed, and broom snakeweed. Typical aster family flowers follow the familiar "composite" pattern of daisies, "composed" of two kinds of flowers. Pull off a "petal" and you discover it's an individual blossom; even without a hand lens, you can see the minute bloom hidden in the incurled base of each ray. In the disk, tiny tubular flowers pack close together, their spiral growth pattern following the Fibonacci number sequence. Broom snakeweed, ubiquitous in the canyon, bears dozens of shirt-button-size yellow daisies on a basketball-size bush; its name comes from the rustle of its dry stems, which can sound like a rattlesnake. In the spring, plants of brittlebush send up their blooms, brilliant yellow daisylike flowers hovering above the rounded gray-green-leaved bush like a bevy of yellow butterflies, the first to waft in the spring.

Variations on the theme are legion, and sometimes they don't look like asters at all. Take skeletonweed, ubiquitous in the canyon. Because it has no disk flowers, its five or six pale pink rays suggest a delicate, simple dianthus. But if you pull off one of the petals, there's that tiny flower inside. Poorweed, with its pungent odor and blue-green foliage, has only disk flowers; sniff the pungent glands on the involucre, a sheath that holds the clusters together (another characteristic of the daisy family). Or arrowweed, the tall, slender, straight-stemmed plants that garnish beaches with their small lavender-pink flowers that look like tiny thistles without the spines. Arrowweed needs frequent rejuvenation from floods. Covered with three feet of sand, it can still vigorously sprout and begin a new stand.

Dan, wonderful botanist on this trip, promises to show me McDougall's flaveria, the modest yellow-flowered shrub that's an aster family endemic. "Endemic" defines a plant or animal that grows only in one specific area and, often, only in one specific habitat, such as on acidic or basic soil. McDougall's flaveria favors Muav Limestone, often near salt springs or seeps. There may be up to ten other endemic plants in Grand Canyon, and they appear as the flora begins to be better researched and identified.

The one Dan shows us grows near a salt seep with maidenhair fern tucked beneath it, flourishing on a Muav Limestone ledge in a kind of aristocratic solitude. In full bloom, six or more quarter-inch-wide bright yellow flowers cluster together at the end of each flowering branch. Flaveria was not identified as a probable endemic until 1975, after herbarium and literature searches were made. As often happens, when botanists really began looking, flaveria turned up elsewhere in similar habitats, the last one only identified a few months before this trip. Dan says it's not been seriously studied and no one knows yet what pollinates it. Grand Canyon is not an easy place to do research.

Pollination in Grand Canyon is a complicated dance, done by completely different species, genera, even families. The moths that bat around your flashlight when you're trying to read at night are generalist pollinators, except for yucca moths: so precise is the fit between plant and pollinator that a specific species of moth pollinates a specific species of yucca. A female yucca moth balls up pollen from one plant and carries it to another, where she lays her eggs in the developing ovary of a single blossom. If too many larvae develop for the food available, the flowers drop prematurely. And to add to the complexity, there's also a fake yucca moth that travels under a false passport, contributing nothing to the pollination cycle.

Up the path above Deer Creek grows a large agave, like the yucca a member of the lily family. Called Anasazi agave, its scientific name, *Agave phillipsiana*, honors Arthur Phillips, a distinguished botanist who has worked in the canyon for many years. Agaves are tall plants, and generally bats pollinate them. When seeds develop they fall to the ground and sprout. But this particular species of agave does not produce seeds but reproduces vegetatively through cloning. That being the case, archaeologists believe that the only way it could have gotten here was to be carried in and planted here specifically for cultivation. Anasazi agave has other advantages: it produces a larger root mass than most agaves do, and its flowering stalk may grow a foot a day. Prehistoric people dug the agave root just before the stalk sprouted to usurp the sugars stored in the plant base. After trimming off the fleshy leaves, they roasted it. Archaeologists find roasting pits throughout the canyon where prehistoric people built a fire, added rocks, and covered them with slices of barrel cactus or prickly pear to protect the root mass and provide moisture for steam. Slow cooking turns the sugars into a palatable food in a process called malting. Prehistoric people enjoyed the cooked gooey center and, of course, anything that sweet can be fermented into an alcoholic beverage, in this case tequila.

A waxy coating covers agave leaves for much the same reason as it does cactus stems: protection from water loss. Cacti practice a different kind of photosynthesis called crassulacean acid metabolism (CAM). The plant's stomata, the pores through which it breathes, are open at night (as opposed to daytime when the stomata of most plants open) when they can take in cooler air and lose less moisture to evaporation. It allows CAM plants to metabolize carbon dioxide in the dark.

Grand Canyon plants are largely desert plants, or at least well adapted to desert conditions. Many plants have narrow leaves, as the ubiquitous coyote willow does, that do not transpire as much as broad leaves. Hairs protect the leaves or stems of many desert plants, making them look gray; hairs cut down on the damaging effects of sunlight and wind, as they do for brittlebush. Evening star, mallow, rock nettle, and brittlebush are all degrees of furry to prickly; evening star leaves have such tenacious hairs that a leaf stuck to your sock will remain firmly attached even through the wash. Many desert plants have a multitude of very tiny leaflets that allow air to circulate between them; many of these belong to the pea family. This permits mesquite and catclaw acacia to withstand high wind as well as high heat.

Ingenious adaptations, clever plants engineering their own survival over time.

I once tended to look at plants only as attractive and fascinating splashes of color and shape that beautify the world. That was before going on a "grocery store walk" with archaeologist Greg Woodall. At the beginning of a group stroll, he points out mesquite pods, plentiful this fall, dangling from the knotted branches like tan icicles. Ground, they form a tasty flour for porridge. Many Indians in the West used the sweetish pulp between shell and bean to make cakes, or brewed the inner bark to make a tea that was often used to treat coughs or lung congestion.

Prickly pears grow all over the dry slopes. Greg says they were probably the most used plants here (their uses were recognized as long ago as 288 BC by Theophrastus, a pupil of Aristotle). Almost every part of the plant is usable: the needles were used for puncturing various materials so they could be sewn together, the flesh could be eaten raw (not particularly recommended—too much oxalic acid) or cooked, and the fruits could be juiced or made into jelly or candy, or chewed like gum. Pads dried and pounded into pulp could be turned into cakes. A settler, at the end of the nineteenth century, described it in rather oxymoronic fashion as a "pleasant diuretic." The pad, roasted and needles removed, was bound warm around the throats of mumps sufferers. An old herbal, delineating prickly pear's myriad uses, makes it sound like a snake oil remedy, good for rheumatism, chronic ulcers, gout, hangnails, and whatever else ails you!

The seeds of four-wing saltbush are full of salts and sodium and come packaged in attractive winged seeds that could be ground into meal. Indians ate the leaves as greens or potherbs, which Greg says was probably the case with any plant that sprouted in the spring after a winter of limited rations. The green leaves, chewed, were good for stomachache; Zuni grind the roots and flowers and moisten them with saliva to make a paste to soothe ant bites.

Whenever I read about medicinal or ceremonial plant use, I am struck by the very specific way in which the plant is used—seeds milled, bark steeped, powders ground, roots dried. Such a huge amount of knowledge has accumulated through trial and, one suspects, sometimes fatal error. A few of the ceremonial plants, like sacred datura, have deadly side effects. To know when and how and how much to use is of crucial importance. Many of these remedies have healed humans for thousands of years, the lore passed down by word of mouth from generation to generation. But now both the tribal wisdom and the plants themselves are disappearing at an alarming rate. Back to Ehrlich again: don't throw away the parts, you might need them someday as a potential cure for modern ailments.

Grasses are plentiful in the canyon. The prevalence of easily harvested seeds makes grasses one of the most nourishing plants on the planet, and native species have been developed into crops all over the world. One of the most beautiful grasses of the Southwest is Indian ricegrass, with a delicate open growth form and threadlike crimped flowering stems. Three-thousand-year-old paintings upstream from Grand Canyon depict Indian ricegrass seed being gathered using seed-beaters and seed bags. The large black seeds are nourishing and easy to harvest, although, some years ago, when I tried to replicate the time necessary to gather seeds, it became obvious to me that finding, picking, and preparing enough for a meal took up most of one's day, unless of course, one had the proper tools at the proper time—what archaeologists call "optimal foraging," or as Greg says, "Getting when the getting's good." Pine dropseed, another delicate grass, is common in the canyon, as is scratchgrass, its feathery heads hazing a slope or growing along streambeds.

But not all grasses are welcome. Meet Ravenna grass. It was brought into Grand Canyon some years ago as an attractive ornamental to plant in the park. And it is handsome, a large bunchgrass of the same genus as sugarcane. It is also a rank and invasive species, and in this river system it reproduces at a rate that would make rabbits retire to their dens in shame. Its feathery heads produce thousands of seeds, which float away by wind and water and can remain viable for more than a single year's growing season, making it a fierce and sneaky competitor. The eradication that began in 1990 was the first done in a programmed way, rooting out plants with shovels, Pulaskis, and hand picks. Now personnel use GPS to pinpoint populations and to recheck to be sure plants are gone. Dan hopes that by the third year Ravenna grass will be a thing of the past.

When Dan asks if I would be interested in stopping at one of the beaches where an eradication crew had done considerable work, I say you betcha. The extermination plot is an unused beach, studded with big rocks. Dan explains that you have to dig up the roots because new plants can sprout from them, and you must decapitate the seed heads and stuff them in a plastic bag because they continue to ripen even when picked and dry, and sprout if they drop to the ground. At this site workers took out about a hundred plants. The good news is that Ravenna grass is one of some 180 invasive plants that may actually be gotten rid of.

Two plants that seem to be here to stay are tamarisk and camelthorn. Tamarisk, another non-native and, like Ravenna grass, brought in as an ornamental around a hundred years ago, clots the banks along the whole river. It can be removed, but it's a huge job, destroying roots, then digging up and dragging the stumps away. Given the number of miles to cover, the slowness of the work, and the quadrillions of seeds just waiting upstream to waft down and even able to sprout in the river itself, it's probably as practical as carrying the Atlantic to the Pacific in a sieve.

Camelthorn, a member of the pea family, appears along the river below the Little Colorado. It grows along roadsides on the rim, and its seeds were likely brought in by one large flash flood, probably in the 1980s. They are a plague on beaches. Their sharp thorns can completely ruin an area for camping. So far it can only be controlled, not eradicated. Camelthorn's seeds hang in pods that act like little boats, flotillas of which spread seeds downriver. Populations formed on sandy beaches also spread by underground runners. They are impervious to herbicides even if such chemicals could be used in the park. Experimental efforts suggest that cutting them several times during the growing season may exhaust them, thereby keeping selected areas open for camping.

Grass in Buck Farm Canyon, Mile 40

At Mile 47R, after an uphill/down-dale dry hike at Saddle Canyon, you reach a cul-de-sac that has remained fairly unchanged in the thirty years I've known it. I've learned to expect a bower of redbuds and Oregon holly and all kinds of small bright blooms, a tiny twinkling stream, a Pacific tree frog on a rock at stream's edge, smiling, and a slender doe poised, as unmoving as if made of ceramic, a figure in a life-size dish garden. The stream hugs the right-hand wall, then morphs into a long narrow pool. A short step up accesses an elegant alcove with a waterfall at the end. The melodic plash of water falling into a tiny pool is pure Respighi, the perfect antidote for a hot day.

But *sic transit gloria mundi*. In the last year a large enough amount of water poured through here to rototill the original streambed and rearrange the drainage. New sprigs colonize gravels that cover a once-grassy sward, repairs on the way. But for now, tangles of debris caught a couple feet up in the shrubs leave a rather slovenly mess.

Later that afternoon, sitting on the beach and looking upstream, the view prompts me to take out watercolors. I reflect, for the thousandth time, that I never truly see a place until I draw it. I've looked at this view a lot of times, but it's not until I put brush or pencil to paper that I mark the differences in character between the two limestones of the Redwall and Muav Formations, displayed clearly on the upstream cliff wall, reminding me of golden afternoons and pleasant journeys. It's the learning that counts, and I learn through my hands as much as my eyes and ears and nose.

I complete three postcard watercolors and two drawings. Trouble is, even a very, very fine pen is too wide to portray those myriad layers, so I pick out a few spots and quirks of rock, figure out characteristic patterns, apologize to the landscape, and just do it. I carry postcard-size watercolor blocks that go quickly. The watercolors lie drying on the beach like leaves dropped from some exotic tree. I learn something with each one. These are not definitive descriptive answers: I know that what I see today will be different from what I will see the next time I sit here. These are not works of art but simply the result of one dabbler's take on a big wall of a canyon at Mile 47R of the Colorado River on a soft summer afternoon around four o'clock.

Around me a handful of people have cameras wedged to their face, looking through the lens for the best view, worrying about composition and light and shutter speed. J. M. W. Turner, the nineteenth-century painter of explosive atmospheric effects, once criticized photographs for being "not true although they may seem so." How Turner would have loved the voluminous space and vibrating colors of Grand Canyon!

A monarch butterfly wafts by on its way south.

One chilling morning I find myself watching the slow progress of sunlight coming down back cliffs, ready for a little warmth on my shoulders. We cluster on the beach to hear Christa Sadler talk about the Butte and Eminence Break Faults. She is a vivid and dynamic teacher, especially when she provides the geologic illustration in full living color right in front of us.

An observant passenger may not note the occasional stutters in otherwise evenly laid rock layers, but even the most geologically uninvolved can't miss

Looking upstream at Saddle Canyon, Mile 47

the big faults that smear up the canyon walls and destroy the continuity of otherwise orderly layers. The Fifty Mile Fault crosses the Colorado, and you can sight the disarray of its passage on both sides of the river, a continuous rumpled landscape of old lithic battles. The Bright Angel Fault, down which the Bright Angel Trail wends, is probably the best known in Grand Canyon because so many people have walked in and out of the canyon on it. The Mohawk-Stairway Fault at Mile 171 has had various names over time; not until 1970 were the names of the two canyons on either side of the river (Stairway right, Mohawk left) joined and hyphenated into one name. The Toroweap Fault crosses the river at Lava Falls Rapid. The Hurricane Fault runs between Mile 191 and 192 before veering off to the south; the Separation Fault spans the river at Separation Rapid, better known as a place of parting for some of J. W. Powell's crew. And finally, the imposing Grand Wash Fault essentially ends Grand Canyon at Mile 276.5.

And that's less than half the faults that cut across or run beside the river. I list these to make a point: Grand Canyon is an active landscape, moving up, down, and sideways, old areas of movement becoming new areas of movement because they provide areas of weakness where molten magma can break through or slumpage can occur. Once established, faults tend to rework themselves, sometimes in rather capricious ways, even to reverse themselves, since less force is required to reactivate an old fault than begin a new one. Big faults spawn a lot of smaller ones, soften the landscape, adjust the levels, round the corners, morph the view into one of those romantic landscapes in disarray painted by Salvator Rosa.

The Eminence Break Fault skirts the great bulge of Point Hansborough at Mile 44. Suddenly, after being walled in, the canyon opens out on the left where the fault cuts close to the river. The wall left, instead of repeating the righteous vertical of Point Hansborough, is slovenly—a room a month after the party of the millennia took place, and no one has come in yet to clean. The lumpy landscape says there may be lots of bodies still under the rugs.

Big faults mean crumbled talus and major breaks in sheer canyon walls, and translate to the few and far between passages in and out of the canyon. When a fault jolts the sequence of beds, it grinds the rock to talus, invites erosion, disturbs solidity, and offers a scrambling ingress or egress from the canyon, or opens access to hidden valleys like Chuar Valley. From Little Nankoweap Creek, at Mile 51.6, to Mile 77 (the beginning of the Upper Granite Gorge), the canyon is markedly influenced by the Butte Fault, which was first a normal fault, dropping 5,000 feet on its western side, and then became a reverse fault, the downside rising 2,700 feet. Chuar Valley over time was uplifted two miles by the Butte Fault, which opened up a huge valley on the right side of the river and brought rock formations to the surface otherwise not visible in the canyon. Canyons cut in the exposed soft rocks, the easily eroded Dox Sandstone and Chuar Group, are broad and bowl shaped, with rounded receding walls, making Chuar Valley one of the magical hikes in Grand Canyon, thanks to the Butte Fault's extravagant movements.

The Upper Granite Gorge begins around Mile 77, cut between walls of Vishnu Schist, as dramatic as a polished sculpture by Henry Moore. Vishnu

Schist is the oldest formation in the canyon, of great density and hardness, formed, melted, reformed, and compressed into an extremely dense rock of a dignified glossy ebony.

Before the original components solidified into Vishnu Schist, they were quartz-rich silts, clays, and sands, washed down toward an early Precambrian sea surrounding the huge supercontinent of Pangaea, one of several times in geologic history that an enormous single continent formed. Between 2.0 and 1.8 *billion* years ago these sediments built beaches and bars along Pangaea's edges and extended its land mass by 50 percent. After this extended shelf formed, a massive volume of volcanic rock surged up through it, and the combined sediments and volcanics built up to an estimated 40,000 feet or more. Subsequent rifting and continental drift eventually broke up Pangaea into separate smaller continents, and the mass of rock that now underlies Grand Canyon was torn lose in that movement. Intense compression, metamorphism, and deformation followed, obliterating much of that first period of movement, and essentially formed the rock that binds this narrow, riotous passageway and causes some seriously mean rapids.

There are few camps in the Inner Gorge, small beaches tucked between black slabs of rock. Camping at Grapevine Rapid at Mile 81.5L, I pitch my tent between two authoritative fins of Vishnu Schist. A spider has strung her web between these two slabs, the total present utilizing the total past. As the spiderweb flutters and twitches, I ponder the immediacy of the moment, played against some of the oldest rock in the world, designed by a river one grain at a time. Worth drawing a poem about.

Hikers in Chuar Valley, Mile 68

On the beach at Phantom Ranch at Mile 87.6R, I hoist myself up onto a shaded bank of Bermuda grass (another non-native) to eat lunch. The beach is a mishmash of boats giving up passengers to walk out the Bright Angel or South Kaibab Trails, picking up passengers walking in, engendering a general desultory wandering about punctuated by "hellos" and "good-byes."

Phantom Ranch, at the base of the two access trails, Bright Angel and South Kaibab, is the main place for people to walk into and out of the canyon for river trips. We have stopped here to pick up five more people that replace the four we lost. Making a transfer is a psychological break. A group that in a very short time has become fairly well annealed into being "old hands" suddenly needs to regroup, start all over. Newcomers hasten to catch up, old hands ride the dynamics of change.

A few violet-green swallows lace the air above the river even though this is a narrower reach of canyon than they usually prefer. Their short stubby bodies soar and skim, dip and swerve, winnowing the air, such sky-breakers and air-sifters. Beaks open, they scoop up gnats and midges, and dip into the river's surface to leave a six-inch line of silver.

I scan the sky and spot a condor floating into view, very high, but clearly a huge bird in steady flight. Prehistoric condors had seventeen-foot wing-spans; the wingspan of present-day condors is eight or nine feet. Condors originally lived in Grand Canyon, evidenced by bone remnants in high remote caves. Modern condors occupied South America and California; when the California population had been reduced to only a few, wildlife researchers removed them from the wild to breed them in captivity, and these chicks form the basis for the Grand Canyon group. The protection

Folds in Vishnu Schist near Clear Creek, Mile 84

of a national park and Grand Canyon's isolation offered an ideal place for the Peregrine Fund to establish a reintroduction program. For years now, teams of observers have manned an observation post *every* day, arriving before dawn and leaving after dark, to keep detailed notes of condor activity, which provides priceless information about condors. This year the first chick fledged, the beginning indication of success.

One of the unexpected challenges with condors has been their interest in and lack of fear of people. When first released, several commonly walked around the South Rim, much to visitors' delight. But being too friendly made them vulnerable, and those who were too friendly were sent back to California for "reeducation" to arm them with a healthy mistrust of humans.

At Monument Creek, five miles plus from Phantom Ranch, I sit on the beach above Granite Rapid at Mile 93.5L. I listen to the rapid's chortling and watch late sunlight bathe the schist cliffs beneath a capping of sunstruck caramel-colored Tapeats Sandstone, glad to be back on the river and away from the confusion of Phantom Ranch. Tantalizing scents of onions frying for fajitas tendril across the beach. A wooden spoon thumping against the side of a bowl portends cake for desert.

While I am peaceably writing, a helicopter grinds over, a sound that chews up the afternoon, the beating of the rotors unnecessarily loud and interruptive. Four to five more copters ratchet across the sky. This camp lies beneath one of the allowed flight paths, so all the activity channels right over our heads. They don't stop until dusk, will begin again at first light. Fie.

I begrudge them their sound and fury. Yes, I understand that this is the only way many people can see the canyon, but what they see is *not* Grand Canyon but a remote, sanitized canyon, no splash, no wind, no gurgling up-wellings, no buzzing cicadas, a soundless rapid on a painted postcard river. An IMAX movie gives a much better picture, *with* sound, and costs a lot less.

When helicopter noises cease, I listen to how water gurgles in a quiet rushing. Every once in a while all the various serpentines and tiny whirlpools join an unwinding upwelling at the same time, and, for a moment, a louder gargling jubilates, celebrating the pleasant rhythm of soporific sounds.

And *now* I can hear the cicadas trill! Yesterday someone found an inch-long impeccably preserved cicada carapace, perfect in every detail of spine and segment of the front legs, neatly unzipped down the back, crawled out of and left to nature to recycle. Tonight I feel as if I sleep inside a Christmas tree, looking out through tamarisk branches to little cicada shells hanging everywhere, like tree ornaments. In this narrow reach of canyon, where the walls are close enough to define the sky, the stars string between them like Christmas lights.

On one very warm summer evening, we camp at Trinity Creek, at Mile 91.5R, a new campsite for me. After dark we walk up the creek, not knowing where we are going until flickering lights ahead promise a time and a place. I feel as if I'm walking into a quiet courtyard in a little Greek village with thick plastered uneven walls, small lighted windows with drawn curtains, a picture leaning against the glass of one window, a branch of a potted tree silhouetted against another. Here we all sit in comfortable silence, all of us villagers, leaning against the warm wall after a long workday in the fields. Comfortable old friends who know one another's histories. In the stillness, Dan's deep voice begins reading Mary Oliver's "Upstream," a beautiful poem that ends, "Attention is the beginning of devotion." With two elders of the village, I walk back through those words to the beach, thinking, "Of course, of course."

A mile and a half before Elves Chasm at Mile 116, someone asks, "Anybody seen Garnet Canyon?" Turns out most of us have not. Worth a stop.

Garnet Canyon does not exit at river level but requires a scramble up a steep wall; once above that, the path strings back away from the cliff and wanders into the small canyon. Battleship rocks rim the horizon; huge Tapeats boulders stud the big rock garden that continues up the draw. An intermittent stream trickles across gravel bars and weaves channels and fills pools, then shimmers on its way. Catclaw acacias cast thin shade. For a while a thick floor of gravel makes sloshy walking. I contour upward under a big overhang of Tapeats Sandstone where I can look up to a ceiling of stains and swirls like those Edvard Munch carved in his wood blocks. Pebbles stuck under ledges at ground level look like peas in a stone pod. A closely layered section of wall sports one eggplant-colored layer, revealing that it was laid down in a reducing environment that contained no oxygen; the eggplant layer is handsomely bound by tan and grey, Navajo rug colors.

Upstream about a hundred yards, two little waterfalls spin out two little streams that hurry down through and over a bumpy ledge, flowing so quickly that you wouldn't see them as they drop into a bathtub-sized pool were it not for their shimmer. The clear water delineates every rock on the gravel bottom, giving them a richer color, a gleaming glamour those around the edges lack. Two sets of white lines scribe the edges of the pools, a foot apart, lacey leftovers of alkali. As I move the only sound is my boots grinding in the gravel and the birdlike chirping of trickling water. Bubbles cluster in the algae, and eighth-inch water striders whiz through their lives, leaving no ripples. I wander higher, passing through layer after layer of rounded Tapeats ledges, stone pillows stacked on top of each other.

Around a corner rises a stunning wall of grayish tan travertine, a common but intermittent phenomenon that marks the left bank of the river from Kwagunt Canyon to Havasu. Being fairly porous, it catches all kinds of rough cobbles, in all kinds of shapes and colors—purple brown, black stripped, polka-dotted, ochre with sage green, rosy quartz, brick red, cream, gray, tan, rosy salmon, off-white. The wall almost qualifies for a mosaic, except the tesserae are disorderly cobbles in wildly assorted sizes and shapes from metate-size to brussels sprout, carelessly jammed together by a busy creator who left almost as many empty holes as filled ones in an unexpected harmony.

The real lagniappe offered by Garnet Canyon is that it does not partake of the overwhelming scale of the big canyon. It is a kindly, human-size space, fairly inaccessible and lightly traveled. In short, a true treasure.

Elves Chasm at Mile 116 might have been designed by an overimaginative set designer except for its access, which requires severe scrambling and shinnying over Volkswagen-size boulders and leaping over a piece of empty space that is akin to hang gliding over a pit of vipers if you're short of shank. But it's worth it. High walls, festooned with maidenhair fern and monkey flowers, protect an idyllic pool, and at the far end a huge alcove holds a ledge at just the right height for the thrill-of-a-lifetime plummet into the pool below. A debris flow in 1984 reamed out the hanging gardens, but they've recovered nicely in the decades since. Plants come and go, but floods will garden here forever.

Just downstream from Elves Chasm at Mile 117.5R is, to my mind, one of the choice camping beaches in the canyon. A spacious sloping dune backs up against numerous Tapeats Sandstone ledge overhangs for protection. Spacious, west-facing for sunsets, shaded in the morning, it offers a magnificent camping space. Mile 117 has only one drawback: whenever I'm there, it rains. As in, *really rains.*

One summer rain chased the raft downstream from Elves Chasm in a gray misty mass that outrowed the raft and pockmarked the sand before our arrival. This afternoon an autumn storm comes straight upstream. Big clouds steamroller toward us, déjà vu all over again. Lightning flickers, thunder explodes two or three miles away. Rain jacket zipped up to my nose, hood battened down, rain hat clamped on top of that, I snuggle into watching the first raindrops hit the river like upside-down tacks, their sharp ends springing into the air the moment they hit, a straight down, no-messing-around kind of rain. It persists until big waterfalls shoot off the high Redwall rim, spew reddened water down a thousand feet, alternately falling as curtains of crystals or plumes of mist. A little thunder, a little lightning, the Colorado's version of *Eine Kleine Nachtmusik*. As I fall asleep, raindrops still pick on the tent with the precision of a metronome. When they finally fade, a spectacular moonrise waltzes its way through ranks of clouds.

I awake to a calm, clear morning. It's not that dawns are any less spectacular than evenings, but in the morning there's the business of getting up, striking tents, packing up, eating breakfast, loading boats, and all of a sudden you're on the river. In the evening there's a psychological ease in unpacking, the tempo slows, my brain gets the message: write now. I make a note to remember that dawn deserves as much attention as evening.

Blacktail Canyon at Mile 120R has a lot of charms, including exquisite acoustics and an up-close-and-personal display of the Great Unconformity.

For years the entrance began on a ledge high above its floor. One ledge-hopped across the Tapeats Sandstone, dropping down into the canyon proper only well past the entrance where the floor of the canyon had risen up to the ledges. A beautiful space unfolded, where huge boulders stood perfectly arrayed to accord with the winding walls, like the gardens at Kyoto. The boulders reflected in pools made lively with dozens of tadpoles and water beetles and dragonfly larvae. Pretty close to flawless.

A few years ago, a flash flood scoured Blacktail and did an imaginative redecorating job that included a new gravel floor. But that was nothing compared to the flash flood last summer. Floodwaters rafted most of the big

Flood over travertine in Elves Chasm, Mile 116

boulders out to the river, filled in the pools, snuffed out the twinkling life they contained, and overlaid everything with at least four feet of gravel. Now you can walk straight up from the river, right on up through the canyon to the last pour-over that effectively blocks you from going any farther.

The Upper Granite Gorge ends at Blacktail, where Tapeats Sandstone descends to near river level. Blacktail is a narrow canyon reamed out along the contact between Cambrian Tapeats Sandstone and the underlying Precambrian Vishnu Schist, two formations separated by 1.2 billion years. Geologists term such a meeting of different rock formations an "unconformity" when younger rocks are separated from much older rocks by erosion and the younger formation rests "unconformably" on the older one below it. Because of the huge amount of time missing here, John Wesley Powell named this meeting the "Great Unconformity." Even the most geologically blasé get silly grins on their faces when it suddenly dawns on them that if they stand with one hand on schist and one hand on sandstone, in the few inches between their handprints they span more than one *billion* years of missing geologic history, the gap between Cambrian and pre-Cambrian worlds.

When I stand here, hands splayed out on rough stone, eyes closed, I find it easy to imagine the wave action of a Cambrian sea sweeping westward some 550 million years ago, crashing into jagged ridges of schist and churning them into pebbles. The sea incorporated these pebbles and cobbles into its sandy beaches that, over time, indurated into Tapeats Sandstone. I work my fingers into the interstices of this cool rough rock that contains all earth's hopes and dreams. I think that if there is any place I can ever come close to glimpsing

Clouds below Blacktail Canyon, Mile 120

the age of this earth, the forces that formed it, the heat that melded it, the seas that overlay it, the time out of mind of sand grains formed, raindrops fallen, breezes wafted, sunshine shafting, all that went on and on in dogged perseverance, millennium after millennium—it is *right* here, *right* now.

The river, past Kanab Creek at Mile 143R, runs dark and viscous. It swirls with cross currents and big boils that heave and belch. A flash flood tore down Kanab Canyon a few hours ago, and now the water runs as thick as fudge sauce. Arm-size branches catch in madly spinning whirlpools or stand straight up on end and raise a fist for help or point hopelessly to the sky. The water is so viscous that no white froth ices the wave tops. The river has totally changed character, and it's ugly. At my feet, the creek runs blood red, as if the cliffs had been split with an ax. Someone slew the dragon up there.

Deer Creek "patio," above Deer Creek Falls at Mile 136.5R, is as magically tranquil as ever—clear rushing water, overwoven sounds, underwoven sounds, sunshine, shadow, leaf patterns casting vibrating shade, watercress, worm casts on the underside of Tapeats Sandstone ledges, coyote willow, baccharis in bloom (with its refreshing witch hazel odor), small waterfalls of all velocities and persuasions, prickly pears on a ridgeline with perfectly arrayed paddles, tiny pebbles to one-ton boulders, all united by the falls' deep continuum that curls up from below.

At this marvelous moment I have the patio all to myself, something that must seldom happen. Without company, I enjoy a private three-ring circus.

By my right knee, one small lizard snuffles across the limestone, ear hole circled in white; above it, a small yellow butterfly and a blue damselfly circle round each other. A western whiptail patters along the ground a few feet away, switching its extravagantly long tail like a flamenco's dancer's dress. Whip-tails prefer terrain like this, where there's some protective vegetation but not enough to hamper their quick running style. The lizard speeds about its tasks like a miniature vacuum cleaner, a busy little life in a vast landscape designed by water and gravity. Another whiptail patters across the Muav pavement, reaches the reclining seep willow, and actually *jumps* almost a foot up into a tangle of debris caught in the willow's stems, noses around, disappears. My jaw drops! I had no idea lizards could do that!

The day turns sultry, and even with my feet in the cool water, I'm too warm. Thinking it may be cooler on the beach, I hike down and find a niche where I can retreat should rain come. The walls form two sides of a triangle bounding a handkerchief-size beach; the third side opens onto the river. I am truly enjoying this solitude, just me and a couple dozen little red ants. I won't invade their territory if they don't invade mine. Their foraging lines fan out, individuals scurrying in all directions. Some scuttle an inch so quickly that they almost seem to jump, then stop, rear up on back legs, sample air with their antennae, continue. When one finds a tidbit, it arrows back home with its contribution. When another brings in an awkward morsel, its housemates immediately join in and attempt to move the load. No huffing and puffing sounds for such an effort, just a lot of shouldering and foot-slipping scram-bling, and no progress. Toting that barge and lifting that bale in unison is not in their limited vocabulary, which communicates simple thoughts, such as "I found food!" but not "You take *that* end and I'll take this." Interesting how much you can do with body language and pheromones, six legs and two antennae, touch and feel, and odor. Such magnificent little clockwork creatures.

Naptime. I arrange my daypack as a headrest, pull my hat over my eyes, luxuriate in the quiet, and doze, mindful that ants don't take naps and that they *do* bite.

Havasu Creek enters the Colorado at Mile 157L. After I scramble and wade and find a good seat and look out across the canyon, the view always reminds me of Seurat's *Sunday Afternoon on the Island of La Grande Jatte*, a big formal painting of Parisians taking the air, done with tiny dots of paint that must have taken forever to complete. There is a static quality in that picture that, for some peculiar reason, always comes to mind at Havasu.

The charm of Havasu lies in its travertine walls and pools formed by the precipitation of calcium carbonate as streams warmed and evaporated. Travertine is a patient process. It encrusts any surface in its way, suffocates sticks and leaves and mosses, drapes over rocks and plants like a blanket, and assumes the form of any object beneath it. Eventually a series of dams forms, over which water pours with velocity sufficient to prevent further plant growth. Travertine creates fairytale places like Elves Chasm and, at Havasu, a Hollywood set for an Esther Williams movie.

I dig out my binoculars to watch a summer tanager flitting about in a low seep willow. Summer tanagers, along with vermilion flycatchers, indigo buntings, great-tailed grackles, and hooded orioles, are one of several birds known to have worked their way up the Grand Canyon corridor since the early seventies after Glen Canyon Dam was completed and riparian habitat developed along the river. Since then summer tanagers have become uncommon but regular summer breeders. The increase in vegetation along the river has provided new habitat for at least one species of mice, and a few amphibians and reptiles have also found new lebensraum in the post-dam environment.

I am content to be here, sitting at rest beside Havasu Creek and watching the magic of rushing water—the creek is booming. I remember in separate detail what it has looked like in times past—full of greenery, bare from flash flooding, neat, messy, what else? This morning? Somewhere in between. On a felled acacia, shoots sprout upward from the horizontal branches. Lots of Bermuda grass. Few velvet ash trees. Lots of trash from past floods interweaves four feet up in tree clusters. The clumps of interwoven branches look so much like an untidy basket that I wonder if that's where the idea first entered the brain of an early basket weaver.

A sacred datura stands out by its erect, authoritative growth pattern, the way it shoves space aside. Dan strolls by on his way to Beaver Falls and stops to look at it. He lifts up a leaf of the bush as gently as nudging a hen off the nest to extract her egg. He points to small round pellets on the ground, the scat of hornworm larvae (also called tobacco worms), robust caterpillars about the size of my little finger. The adults are better known as sphinx or hummingbird moths for their size and habit of hovering. They can hang in front of a big datura bloom, wings whirring like an electric fan, and unroll a long proboscis that uncoils like a watch spring and through which they siphon up nectar. These moths and their caterpillars coevolved with sacred datura; ethnobotanist Gary Nabhan identifies them as the "only creatures known" that can consume the poisonous components of sacred datura and survive, although even they can get woozy if they imbibe too much. Like monarch butterfly caterpillars that incorporate milkweed toxins in their bodies, hornworms' uptake gives them protection from predators. "Don't even think about fingering a leaf, forgetting, and then rubbing your eyes," warns Dan, and goes on his way.

A wise warning, for sacred datura packs a seriously poisonous package of chemicals, atropine and scopolamine, substances always used in carefully controlled doses, because in uncontrolled doses they are often fatal. Ophthalmologists often use atropine to dilate eyes during examination. Being both poisonous and narcotic, it has often been used in native ceremonies to produce hallucinations or delirium. The fat-soluble tropane alkaloids of scopolamine are absorbed by the skin and produce hallucination. I once wore a too generous scopolamine patch behind my ear for seasickness and discovered that I could not take notes or write in a straight line until well after I removed the patch. Obviously prehistoric people who used sacred datura in rituals were aware of precisely how much to use and for what effects.

Some sacred datura buds unfurl like five-pointed pinwheels, getting ready for this evening's dance of hummingbird moths. Other plants with nascent buds, some with last year's prickly seed pods, flourish in the sand. In bloom, datura's triumphant trumpets burst on the vision, fragrant flowers that open to the sky, pure of line, innocent and white, but true *fleurs du mal*.

On the shaded side of Havasu Creek, I sit beneath a huge Muav overhang where rock scales off the wall like cornflakes, and where I'd hoped to be cooler than I am—my thermometer has just crept into three digits. But there's a good bench to sit on where I can comfortably write, and I'm thankful for the shade when I look directly across the creek to the barren sun-split walls. Close by, grapevines loop all over the ground and any obstacle, messy with browned leaves. On the end of a catclaw acacia branch, a robber fly clings, poised to attack any handy victim. A cinnabar-colored dragonfly helicopters in to alight on another branch. I find myself smiling: I treasure this time to watch E. O. Wilson's "little things that run the world" run the world.

After Havasu, as the night shall follow the day, comes Lava Falls at Mile 179. A rapid I'd be happy never to run again, Lava Falls is an ugly heap of water, without grace or beauty, a sledgehammer on the loose.

Debris flows from Prospect Canyon slammed Volkswagen-size boulders clear across the river and built Lava Falls. "Debris flow" is not a particularly familiar term in the rim world. A debris flow is an all-at-once rambunctious onslaught of rock and mud bludgeoning pell-mell down a canyon, a flash flood with an attitude. Debris flows formed most of the big rapids in the river and continue to do so. Humans seldom see debris flows since they tend not to send out timetables, but once seen they evoke awestruck comments.

Because I am not a masochist, I stay aboard when we pull over to scout

Datura in bloom at Havasu, Mile 183

Lava Falls. I do not need to see this maelstrom again. Instead I watch two trains of cumulonimbus mammatus clouds float over Prospect Canyon, remnants of a dying cumulus cloud. Their turbulence is framed by the canyon walls, my turbulence framed by fear and loathing.

Face it, in practical terms, running Lava is the only way I'm going to get downstream. It strikes me as boating on the River Styx without a paddle, swimming the Hellespont without a life jacket, surviving the Drake Passage in a canoe, struggling between Charybdis and Scylla, all combined. The dull sun casts a thoughtless shadow. I wait for the anesthetic of motion, leaving shore, getting through. Grant me a clear mind and a pure heart in this breathless quest for survival, life without waves, quiet walks, Puccini operas, e-mail, front doors, 37-cent stamps, all the commonalities of my life . . .

Our skilled boatman navigates Lava Falls in minutes, and a decade later we pull over to a warm springs gushing out of the rocks below on river left. Nothing to it—piece of cake. Two pieces of cake. Warm water. Sigh. It's over.

Below Lava Falls black basalt begins to coat the canyon walls in earnest. The area between the Grand Wash and the Hurricane-Toroweap fault systems is riven with small faults, forming areas of weakness where lava escaped through cinder cones or fissures. Most of the lava flows originated on the right side of the river, and many formed dams whose remnants still cover the walls; one that formed at Prospect Canyon backed water all the way up into Utah. The result of all these flows is an architectural canyon, draped like a catafalque with handsome black lavas.

One of most beautiful exposures of basalt in Grand Canyon is at Mile 183, where boaters have an end-on view of basalt columns spread like fans. When lava cools, joints develop at cool points from which these fractures commonly form 120 degrees apart, and the result is these hexagonal columns. The faster the cooling, the finer the columns. These unusually slender columns have an elegance, an Art Deco quality, a finely pleated dancer's black silk skirt unfurling in air stirred by movement. This wall is always something I'd like to take some time to look at—but the boat always goes by too quickly and never stops. Never a chance to touch that smooth black rock, identify the tufted little bowling-ball gray-green bushes tucked in the cracks like cloves in a baked ham, to visit the barrel cactus with iridescent red spines, never an hour to look around, never a day to explore the columns, wondering if this sculptural screen could have been moved here from sculptor Louise Nevelson's studio.

Evidence continues downstream of significant volcanic activity. We row past a wall of double tiers of columns, narrow above, larger below. The magnificent wall goes on a hundred yards or so. When I type up my field notes later, I find I have entered "Beautiful, beautiful" more than once.

Last night there were hundreds of stars set in a deep blue-black sky, patterns perceived by ancient navigators thousands of years ago, lighting passages to who knows where. Venus sat below and to the right of a bright waning moon. The sky lightens. A tiny bat still hunts. Stars fade. Only a moon and a planet. Venus fades. Only a moon. Moon fades. Only a sky. And now there are cliffs, promontories, colors, operatic sets with an orchestra full of clarion trumpets and sonorous cellos and wild crescendos. Another world. In tracking this subtle progression, I keep my promise to the dawn.

On this morning of leaving, clouds tile the sky in little irregular squares, like an Escher drawing, ready to segue into humpback chub. We agree to a silent float from camp at Mile 202R to takeout at Diamond Creek at Mile 226. The sky is in a lot better shape than it has been recently, a true pale blue with fewer, smaller clouds, more diaphanous, more fleeting, the last gasp of whatever storm brought them in to plague our days. The outliers went on to a big party somewhere south; the stragglers remain behind, drying out after a few days of debauchery. Diamond Peak appears shortly below Mile 221, its summit at the same elevation as Lees Ferry, a measure of how far we've descended, then disappears at a turning in the canyon.

Over the years one becomes sensitized to the subtle changes that take place as a trip as memorable as this draws to a close, as if a change in scenery portends a change in dynamics. At first, I found the leavings difficult because I didn't know if I'd ever come back. I had not yet learned to make the transition. Now I float gently in that hammock between one reality and another. All the new experiences and new knowledge are rolled up like a pair of sandy socks in my duffle. I've learned that if I don't record them, I won't recall the clamorous rain, the routine for meals, or remember to leave clean dishes in a Clorox rinse for half a minute, using a foot pump instead of a faucet—nuisances in the rim world but down here a necessity and a point of pride.

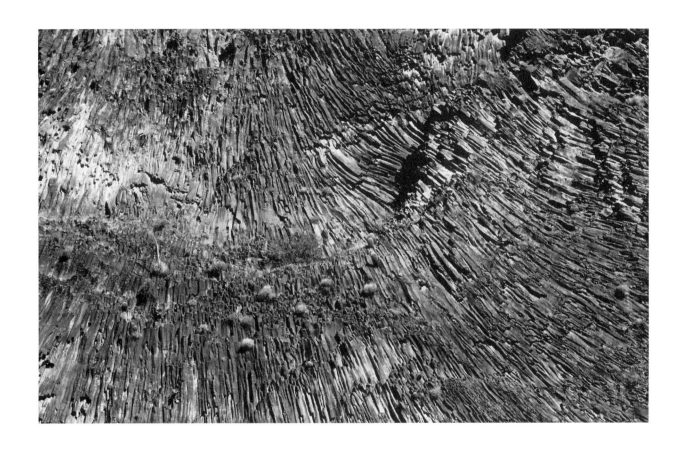

Columnar basalt below Lava Falls, Mile 183

We promise to keep in touch by e-mail, but it won't be the same, the easy camaraderie congealed by electronics to something else. There will be moments of nostalgia for a life both simpler and more complex, and flashes of vivid experience like running Crystal or the shock of four feet of gravel at Blacktail, an overlaid grid of memories superimposed on a quotidian life, the sliding passage of one day to the next, a splashing, flowing, harmonious life punctuated by periods of galloping terror.

Life on the river keeps us a little more alert, grants a little more balance, assurance. It blesses us with a chance to contemplate our place in time and space, to look at an abundant natural world in great working order and feel reassured by the little things that winnow the air and hide under ground cloths and crawl up stems to shed skins, of the hairy or spiny or thorny plants that bloom with such passion. Maybe that's something to take away from a time like this—a reassurance of life and living that comes with reestablishing our link with a heartening natural world, recognizing the beneficence and rectitude and unmitigated honesty of an environment that works by rules that join plant, animal, and mineral. It's understanding the order and chance that combine for such rich surroundings: the vivid blue of a canyon sky, the song the river sings to each of us, and the bright stars that are like good deeds in a naughty world. After all's said and done, life here is a respite, a chance to regroup, learn to tie a bowline, appreciate a flower, welcome new thoughts and ideas, reestablish connection to the natural world. An arrowweed branch, rocking in the morning breeze, reminds me of a metronome and its insistent ticking of time, reminds me to give thanks for one more day on the river.

Hikers at Mile 214

Give me this day my daily river, and let me keep these realizations tucked in a pocket along with some freeloading sand, a lizard footprint, a cicada carapace, a scrap of sky, sunburned hands, and faith in the health and wealth of the natural world. And in this river that always runs downhill.

bibliography

Beus, Stanley S., and Michael Morales. 1990. *Grand Canyon geology.* New York: Oxford University Press; Flagstaff: Museum of Northern Arizona.

Brian, Nancy. 1992. *River to rim: A guide to place names along the Colorado River in Grand Canyon from Lake Powell to Lake Mead.* Flagstaff, AZ: Earthquest Press.

Euler, R. C. 1984. The archaeology and geology of Stanton's cave. In *The archaeology, geology, and paleobiology of Stanton's Cave,* ed. Robert Euler, 7–32. Grand Canyon Natural History Association, Monograph 6. Grand Canyon National Park, AZ.

Fradkin, Philip L. 1981. *A river no more: The Colorado River and the West.* New York: Knopf.

Grand Canyon National Park. 2004. Draft Environmental Impact Statement: Colorado *River Management Plan*. Grand Canyon, AZ: National Park Service. Also available at http://www.nps.gov/grca/crmp (accessed May 2, 2005).

Hamblin, W. Kenneth, and J. Keith Rigby. 1968. *Guidebook to the Colorado River. Part 1, Lees Ferry to Phantom Ranch in Grand Canyon National Park*. Provo, UT: Dept. of Geology, Brigham Young University.

———. 1969. *Guidebook to the Colorado River. Part 2, Phantom Ranch in Grand Canyon National Park to Lake Mead, Arizona-Nevada*. Provo, UT: Dept. of Geology, Brigham Young University.

Krutch, Joseph Wood. 1958. *Grand Canyon: Today and all its yesterdays*. New York: Morrow.

Lavender, David. 1985. *River runners of the Grand Canyon*. Tucson: University of Arizona Press.

Leydet, Francois. 1964. *Time and the river flowing*. San Francisco: Sierra Club.

Martin, Russell. 1989. *A story that stands like a dam: Glen Canyon and the struggle for the soul of the West*. New York: Holt.

McDougall, W. B. 1964. *Grand Canyon wild flowers*. Flagstaff, AZ: Museum of Northern Arizona and Grand Canyon Natural History Association.

Oliver, Mary. 2004. Upstream. In *Blue Iris: Poems and Essays*. Boston: Beacon Press.

Powell, J. W. 1875. *Exploration of the Colorado River and its canyons*. Washington, DC: Smithsonian Institution, 1981.

Ryan, Kathleen, ed. 1998. *Writing down the river*. Flagstaff, AZ: Northland Press.

Simmons, George C., and David L. Gaskill. 1969. *Marble Gorge and Grand Canyon*. Flagstaff, AZ: Northland Press in cooperation with the Powell Society Ltd.

Stanton, R. B. 1968. *Down the Colorado*. Ed. D. L. Smith. Norman: University of Oklahoma Press.

Stegner, Wallace. 1954. *Beyond the hundredth meridian*. Boston: Houghton Mifflin.

Stevens, Larry. 1983. *The Colorado River in Grand Canyon: A guide*. Flagstaff, AZ: Red Lake Books.

Stone, Julius F. 1932. *Canyon country*. New York: G.P. Putnam's Sons.

Thayer, Dave. 1986. *A guide to Grand Canyon geology along Bright Angel Trail*. Grand Canyon, AZ: Grand Canyon Natural History Association.

Webb, Robert H. 1996. *Grand Canyon, a century of change: Rephotography of the 1889–1890 Stanton Expedition*. Tucson: University of Arizona Press.

Zwinger, A. H. 1995. *Downcanyon*. Tucson: University of Arizona Press.

about the author

Ann Zwinger grew up on a river in Indiana, and western rivers have flowed through her life and writing in *Run, River, Run* and *Downcanyon*, as well as in numerous essays on the San Juan. She collaborated with her nature writer daughter, Susan, on *Women in Wilderness*, an anthology of women's nature writing. She also writes and illustrates the deserts and mountains of the West, more interested in plants than animals because "plants stand still to be drawn." She is an instructor and vice chair of Grand Canyon Field School, and adjunct professor at Colorado College where she teaches "Writing the Natural History Essay."

about the photographer

Michael Collier is a freelance photographer, writer, pilot, and family physician who lives in Flagstaff, Arizona. After receiving degrees in geology from Northern Arizona University and Stanford University, he rowed boats commercially on the Colorado River in the Grand Canyon. Among his other books are *Floods, Droughts, and Climate Change* (with Robert H. Webb) and *A Land in Motion: California's San Andreas Fault*.

Library of Congress Cataloging-in-Publication Data

Zwinger, Ann.

    Grand Canyon / Ann H. Zwinger and Michael Collier.— 1st ed.

      p. cm. — (Desert places)

    Includes bibliographical references.

    ISBN-13: 978-0-8165-2432-7 (pbk. : alk. paper)

    ISBN-10: 0-8165-2432-7 (pbk. : alk. paper)

    1. Grand Canyon (Ariz.)—Description and travel. 2. Grand

Canyon (Ariz.)—Pictorial works. 3. Natural history—Arizona—

Grand Canyon. I. Collier, Michael, 1950- II. Title. III. Series.

F788.Z85 2006

917.91'32—dc22

                                   2005028391